REACHING YOUR SUMMIT

REACHING YOUR SUMMIT

SOME THINGS YOU CAN ONLY SEE FROM THE TOP

BY
CASEY TREAT

Harrison House
Tulsa, Oklahoma

Reaching Your Summit—
Some Things You Can Only See From the Top
ISBN 1-57794-212-4
Copyright © 2000 by Casey Treat
Christian Faith International
P. O. Box 98800
Seattle, Washington 98198

Published by Harrison House, Inc.
P. O. Box 35035
Tulsa, Oklahoma 74153

It shall come to pass in the latter days that the mountain of the Lord's house shall be firmly established as the highest of the mountains, and shall be exalted above the hills, and all nations shall flow to it.

And many people shall come and say, Come, let us go up to the mountain of the Lord, to the house of the God of Jacob; that He may teach us His ways and that we may walk in His paths.

Isaiah 2:2,3 AMP

CONTENTS

CONTENTS

INTRODUCTION

I want you to join me in studying the mountains God mentions in the Bible. God did some exciting and powerful things on *mountains!*

The Lord likes mountains. He calls them "the holy hills." And of course, the city of Jerusalem, the city of God, is nestled in the midst of several mountains.

We are going to study some great events that have happened on various mountains mentioned in the Bible as well as events that are yet to happen on them.

The Lord ascended from the Mount of Olives, and He is coming back to that same mountain when He returns for His Body of believers. So we need to be plugged in to what the Lord has done, what He is doing, and what He wants to do on the mountain—His place of quiet for communing and fellowshipping with you.

I believe there is a physical, natural interpretation for some of the things that happened on mountains. But more importantly, there is a spiritual significance. It's an impression. A symbol. A word picture that should impact our lives.

We can learn from this, and move up in our walk with God. I know I have, particularly from our location in Seattle, where we are in the midst of some of the greatest, most amazing and astounding mountains in the world. We can learn spiritual lessons when we plug into how to reach the summit of the destiny God has ordained for each of us. I want to use the analogy of my recent climb up Mount Rainier to understand our spiritual "climb" in the Lord.

At the end of each chapter you will find a "Personal Application of Summit-Climbing Truths" section that will reinforce the biblical principles presented in that chapter.

My prayer for you is that you will leave the low life of mediocrity and climb your "destiny mountain" to the high life—the superabundant life, the over-and-above-all-you-dare-ask-or-think kind of life that God has prepared for you! (Eph. 3:20 AMP.)

—*Casey Treat*

PART 1

SETTING YOUR SIGHTS ON A HIGHER SPIRITUAL PLANE

CHAPTER ONE

CLIMBING THE MOUNTAIN
OF TRANSFORMATION

Let's look first at Matthew 17:1-9, in which Jesus was transfigured on a high mountain before three of His disciples.

> Now after six days Jesus took Peter, James, and John his brother, led them up on a high mountain by themselves; and He was transfigured before them. His face shone like the sun, and His clothes became as white as the light.
>
> And behold, Moses and Elijah appeared to them, talking with Him.
>
> Then Peter answered and said to Jesus, "Lord, it is good for us to be here; if You wish, let us make here three tabernacles: one for You, one for Moses, and one for Elijah."
>
> While he was still speaking, behold, a bright cloud overshadowed them; and suddenly a voice

came out of the cloud, saying, "This is My beloved Son, in whom I am well pleased. Hear Him!" And when the disciples heard it, they fell on their faces and were greatly afraid.

But Jesus came and touched them and said, "Arise, and do not be afraid." When they had lifted up their eyes, they saw no one but Jesus only.

Now as they came down from the mountain, Jesus commanded them, saying, "Tell the vision to no one until the Son of Man is risen from the dead."

After Jesus had risen from the dead, the disciples began to tell about His transfiguration. They wrote about it in the gospel accounts so we can read about it today. This event, which took place *on a mountain*, has important implications for us today regarding:

- The glory of God.

- The glory of divinity.

- The deity of God that radiated from Jesus.

- The visitation of Moses and Elijah.

- The law and the prophets' meeting with the Son of God.

- The grace of God combining the law and the prophets into a new covenant, the New Testament.

- The disciples and how this event affected their lives.

Notice, it all took place on a mountaintop. There are many things Jesus would not do on the normal level of life where everyone else lived. There were many things the Lord wanted people to experience, but He would not let them experience it if they weren't willing to climb a mountain with Him, so to speak. At times, even the multitudes were asked to climb to a higher place. Then Jesus would sit down and teach them.

The *natural* significance is that the Lord was trying to get up where the multitudes could see Him as He taught, because they did not have arenas and coliseums, sound systems and microphones. He had to get to a place where the multitudes could see and hear Him.

The *spiritual* significance is that if you want to live in the low life, there are things from God you will never have. If you want to dwell where everyone else dwells, there are things from God you will never hear. If you are not willing to put forth the effort to get out of your normal circumstances, break out of your routine and get up above the low level of "average"—what the world calls "normalcy"—there are things that God will never be able to accomplish in your life.

Climbing takes effort. It's not always fun. Sometimes it's hard work. But when you begin to climb, suddenly you begin to see things you've never seen before. Your vision gets better. The air gets cleaner and clearer. And you can see all kinds of new paths opened up to you.

MY CLIMB UP MOUNT RAINIER

So climbing a mountain can be a very spiritual and powerful experience.

In an effort to be able to teach this with more authority, I climbed Mount Rainier recently. I spare no expense to bring you the illustrative facts! I spare no effort to bring to you the reality of the principles of God's Word. I climbed a mountain to see if I could learn anything to enlighten you in *your* climb to the summit of your destiny.

A team of eight people from my church, Christian Faith Center in Seattle, joined me climbing Mount Rainier. Three of them were experienced mountain climbers.

We left from Paradise Lodge and climbed up to the summit of Mount Rainier. Paradise is situated at an elevation of 5,000 feet, and the summit is close to 14,500 feet. We left Paradise with forty-pound backpacks containing tents, food, water, ropes, crampons, safety supplies and so forth for the three days and two nights we would spend on the mountain.

We had been preparing for this trip for seven months. The funny thing about climbing a mountain is that it seems as if you are tired from the moment you start. I mean, about an hour outside of Paradise I'm thinking, *Are we there yet?* (I kept looking for the guys who help carry the stuff, but I couldn't find them!) You realize right away that the process is going to be long. The days are going to be long. It's not necessarily going to be that much fun, but you do it for the reward of accomplishing a goal and reaching the summit.

So the first lesson we learned was that *you must keep going, take just one more step and just keep on keeping on!*

The first night in the tent, we were between 9,000 and 9,500 feet. It was freezing cold. The wind blew all night long. This was not the Four Seasons Hotel! It wasn't even a Motel 6. On a 20-foot ledge on the side of Mount Rainier, we found a little level spot in the snow, pitched our tents and tried to make it through the night. We could see all the way to Mount Hood in Oregon. The next day we went on up to Camp Hazard—which is at about 11,000 feet—where we spent the night. Then on the third day, we hit the summit.

On the first part of the trip, you think, *I'm not going to make it. I don't think I can get there!*

I was convinced by the end of the first day that I probably wouldn't make it. By the second day, I was *sure* I wouldn't make it. But the guys leading the team had confidence in us, and that kept us going.

The third morning we were totally wasted. Some of us had altitude sickness. We were trying to force food down each other, because you simply don't feel like eating.

But you learn a great lesson in the process. On the way to the summit, you come to a point where you realize that because others believe in you and because you have gone through so much pain, you're not about to quit before you get to the top. You just keep going.

On the third day, teams of three were roped together. We had been trained so that if one person fell, the other two would self-arrest. In other words, you hit the ice with ice axes and crampons to hold the fallen friend.

The summit looked so close, but it didn't come quickly. It took another hour or more to reach it. You keep going by taking one more step.

And how do you reach the summit of your destiny? The same way: By taking one more step. By talking things out one more time. By forgiving one more time. By accepting one more time.

Let me give you another example. How do you "grow" a business? You show up for work one more day. You make one more sale. You keep going one more week.

Our church, Christian Faith Center, has never done anything fast. We've just kept on going. We reach one more person, air one more broadcast, help start one more church, hold one more Sunday service.

And that's precisely how you get to the summit! *You take one more step!* It never gets easier, and it may never feel better. You may feel miserable and ask yourself, "Why am I doing this?"

But there is one thing I noticed while climbing up the mountain. There was no one else around but our team! Not too many folks ever get to see that view. Not too many people make the effort and get to enjoy that place.

A few will climb to the summit. A few will go through the pain. A few will go through the effort. A few will do what it takes to get to the top.

However, a lot of Christians never experience a deep, powerful, profound relationship with God. Most people are willing to settle for a low-level relationship with God.

In any case, exhausted though we were in struggling to reach the summit, after about fifteen minutes of praying in tongues, we were renewed and revived. Climbing a mountain will make you pray, that's for sure. We made it to the summit, which is approximately 14,500 feet. The air was so thin that you had to take four or five breaths to get one good breath!

But we began to rejoice and celebrate. We began to thank God—until we realized what no one had told us: We had to go back down Mount Rainier! I was looking for a helicopter. I got out my little cell phone and called my wife. I said, "Wendy, I made it! Send a helicopter!"

We were praising God, rejoicing and thanking Him when suddenly someone else showed up and joined us. He came up the mountain from the other side with another group. His teammates didn't make it all the way, so he figured he'd better find someone to rejoice with.

I'm talking about membership, fellowship, leadership and discipleship.

But we weren't done. The vision wasn't over. Now we had to go back down Mount Rainier. That was about ten o'clock in the morning. We spent the rest of the day going back down the mountain.

In this climb up Mount Rainier, I learned so much about myself and the other climbers. You see so much more in other people when they are climbing, and you see so much more in yourself than you knew was there.

DON'T SETTLE FOR A MEDIOCRE CLIMB!

You know, Jesus took three of His disciples and led them up on a high mountain. Are you willing to do what Jesus did and go to that higher place by yourself to hear what God wants to say to you? To see what God will do with you? To see what is really in you? It's so easy to settle into a mundane lifestyle—the regular routines and a just-get-by, hang-in-there mentality. Too many of us settle for this type of lifestyle.

One of the reasons I prepared for seven months to climb Mount Rainier was that I wanted to get out of my regular routine. And since then I have made a commitment that I will regularly do something that I've never done before. I will get out of my routine, out of my everyday life, out of my "couch potato" maintenance mentality and go beyond myself. On a regular basis, I will do something that challenges me in my spirit, soul and body—something I've never done before. You see, I don't want to be the average human being who spends his life using 5 percent of his brain and about that much of his strength.

When was the last time you did something for the first time? When was the last time you discovered something about yourself that you didn't know was there?

Jesus led three disciples to a high mountain because He wanted to show them something that they did not know before.

When people settle for the easy way, the worldly way, the maintenance way, the survival way—or even when they settle for "the norm"—they never find out what is really in them.

Many times you hear athletes say, "You don't know what you've really got inside you until you come up against a team that challenges you to the max."

As a Christian, you'll never know what you and God can do together until you get to a higher place, until you fight for a higher relationship, until you reach for higher goals, until you press for a higher life.

Part of the reason that I climbed Mount Rainier is that I want to live in the Spirit this way every day. I want to find out what's available and what God really can do with me.

It may be only when we get to heaven that we will get a glimpse of the potential we wasted on the earth. Perhaps only then will we realize what we could have done.

Instead of pressing for a higher life, maybe we whined about how we didn't have time or couldn't afford to do something. Or maybe we said we were so tired and no one would help us. But in heaven, we will recognize all of our excuses for a mediocre, maintenance, survival, mundane, routine, just-get-by life.

As you read this book, I pray that you will begin to see that there is a higher level of life. There is a greater experience—a greater adventure—for you in God. You can have the relationship with Him that you have wanted but not yet experienced. You can experience a transfiguration, a transformation that God wants to do in you if you will climb to that place. The Lord is waiting to meet you there!

PERSONAL APPLICATION OF SUMMIT-CLIMBING TRUTHS

1. I will climb above the mediocrity of a "low life" and strive to reach a higher level of life in Jesus Christ by

   _____

   _____

   _____

   _____

2. I am preparing for a spiritual climb to higher heights in the Lord by _____

   _____

   _____

   _____

3. A mountain climber's backpack usually contains food, water, tents, safety supplies, crampons and so forth. My spiritual backpack contains_____

   _____

   _____

   _____

4. I will go beyond a "couch potato," maintenance mentality and challenge myself regularly to achieve higher goals by _____

    _____

    _____

    _____

CHAPTER TWO

JESUS WENT TO A HIGHER PLACE TO RECEIVE FROM GOD

We will look at several Scriptures that show us how often Jesus went to a mountain to pray, receive from God, move to a higher place in God or accomplish the next step in His ministry. If Jesus had to "go to the mountain" to pray, you and I are going to have to do it too.

Matthew 5:1-2 says:

> **And seeing the multitudes, He went up on a mountain, and when He was seated His disciples came to Him.**
>
> **Then He opened His mouth and taught them.**

The multitudes were at a lower level. Jesus wanted to see who really wanted to be a disciple, who really wanted to come up after Him, hear the truths and receive the deeper things of God. So He walked a little bit higher on the mountain, sat down and began to teach what became known as the Sermon on the Mount. (Matt. 5-7.)

CLIMB A LITTLE HIGHER

Some of Jesus' most profound teaching couldn't be heard by the people in the city streets or those living down in the valleys. It couldn't be heard by the average, everyday person. Only those who were willing to go up a little higher, climb a little farther and take the time, effort and pain to push through the challenges and climb the mountain heard it.

Matthew 14:23 says, **When He had sent the multitudes away, He went up on the mountain by Himself to pray. Now when evening came, He was alone there.**

You see, you have to find a place where you can be alone with God. Jesus sent the crowds away. He sent everyone away—even His best friends, the disciples—and went up on a mountain to pray. This verse says, **He was alone there.** Where do you go to be alone with God? Where do you go to reach that higher place? That deeper place? I'm not necessarily talking about a physical place, although it takes that sometimes. But how do you get to that "mountain-top" in your spirit where it's just you and God?

If we want that intimacy, that relationship and that power from heaven, we've got to follow Jesus' example: He went to the mountain alone.

Matthew 15:29-30 says:

> **Jesus departed from there, skirted the Sea of Galilee, and went up on the mountain and sat down there.**
>
> **Then great multitudes came to Him, having with them the lame, blind, mute, maimed, and many others; and they laid them down at Jesus' feet, and He healed them.**

How do you get the power to heal the lame, the blind, the mute, the maimed? You spend a night on the mountain.

How do you get what it takes to meet the needs of the people around you? How do you go to work all day, be a good husband or wife, take care of your kids, coach the little league team and still have energy enough for your wife or husband? How do you do it? You get up on that mountain and spend some time alone with God.

Then, when the multitudes show up—those you call family—you will be ready for them.

Oftentimes, we get burned out because we're trying to work, manage a family, volunteer and handle church. And everything starts to become so stressful that we don't take time to pray. We don't take the time to go to the mountain and be alone with God.

So then we have not only the stress of the world but we have disconnected from the power source! Folks, the problem is not that we don't have time to pray; we don't have time *not* to pray.

A great preacher once said, "I'm so busy today, and there is so much on my schedule that I'm going to take an extra hour and pray."

But what do we usually say? "I'm so busy today, I've got so much on my schedule, I'll pray in the car on the way to the office."

It's great to pray in the car. That's better than getting mad at everybody around you! But don't ever take the attitude that you don't have time to pray, because when you stop praying, you disconnect from the very source of what you need.

The way Jesus prepared for the multitudes who came with all their diseases, pains and problems was to find a place on the mountain where He could be alone to commune with God.

Whether that's in your living room, your backyard, your camper or your closet, find a mountain somewhere where it's just you and God.

THE JERUSALEM MOUNTAINS— A SITE OF GREAT SPIRITUAL ACTIVITY

Matthew 24:3 says, **Now as He sat on the Mount of Olives, the disciples came to Him privately, saying, "Tell us, when will these things be? And what will be the sign of Your coming, and of the end of the age?"** So Jesus began to talk to them about the last days.

When Jesus ascended after the crucifixion, it was from the Mount of Olives, and He will descend to that same mount at the Second Coming.

I have been to the Mount of Olives—a mountain outside the city of Jerusalem. From the mountain, you can see the walls in various parts of the city. And nearby is an olive grove. That's why they call it the Mount of Olives.

Jerusalem itself is located at about 2,000 feet above sea level, settled in the midst of several hills.

When I think of mountains, I think of Rainier, Adams and Baker in Washington state and Hood in Oregon, which are many thousands of feet high. But in Jerusalem the foothills are 2,000 to 3,000 feet high—only about 200 to 300 feet above the valleys.

Many spiritual things took place on Jerusalem mountaintops: Moses received the Law, Elijah talked with God, Jesus talked with God.

Just outside the city is Golgotha, the mount where Jesus was crucified.

When you're in Jerusalem, you can see all these mountains, because Israel is a very mountainous region. When you go north up to the Sea of Galilee, there are mountains all around.

Throughout the Bible, you read about the holy hill, Mount Zion, where Jerusalem is located. The mountains declare the glory of God. God is in the mountains, and He does a lot there.

Go for the Top!

Are you one God could call up to the mountain? Or are you one stuck living in the valley? God wants to meet us, teach us and lift us up in His glory on the mountain, which means we've got to be willing to climb up there. We've got to be willing to go for it. We can't settle for life in the lowlands.

What kind of person are you? One who looks at Mount Rainier and wonders what it would be like to be up there? Or one who actually climbs up Mount Rainier and experiences it?

Another reason I climbed Mount Rainier is that when I was a small child, almost every weekend my family would drive up to Mount Rainier and stay at some little park near the mountain. My grandfather always pointed it out to me and said, "Look at that mountain. Wow!"

I was just a little kid, but I got tired of hearing about it. I thought, *What's the big deal?* But his comment got inside me. Somehow my grandfather affected me. So now, as a father, every time we drive down the road, I see the mountain and say to my children, "Look at that mountain!" They talk to me just like I used to talk to my grandpa. "Yup, it's still there!" they say.

I think my grandfather taught me that appreciation as a small child because he recognized the glory and the majesty of God in Mount Rainier.

One day I said, "Someday I am going to stand on top of that mountain!" Now, forty some years later, I *have* stood on the top of that mountain! I have a whole new view now. Every time I look at it, not only can I see the view from the ground, but I can visualize the view from the summit as well.

You have to decide, *Am I going to be one who stands on the top, or am I going to be one who always wonders what it would be like to stand on the top?* I'm not talking about the physical experience, because who cares whether you ever go up there in the natural or not? I'm talking about your attitude toward life and the experiences of life.

This life is not a rehearsal, folks. This is it. You get one life. No practice. Live it to the max. Are you going to be the one who climbs the mountain to be the kind of husband or wife God wants you to be? Are you going to *wonder* what it would be like to have a family that is blessed by God, or are you going to go ahead and have that family with the blessing of God? Are you going to *wonder* what it would be like to have the faith of God in your company and in your business and serve God every day of your life, or are you going to be the one who does it?

When the hand of God is on your life, that sets the stage for leadership, relationship and prosperity.

You can look at the mountain and wonder what it would be like to be up there. Or you can decide to climb it, stand on top and experience it.

And for every promise of God, there are people who look at the promise and wonder what it would be like to experience it. Then there are those who climb up and get the promise. *Let's go up and check it out,* they say. *Let's not just hear about it and look at it. Let's experience it for ourselves.*

EXPANDING YOUR VISION

I've given you several Scripture examples in which Jesus went to the mountain to experience something supernatural and people went with Him to hear something supernatural.

Matthew 26:30 says, **And when they had sung a hymn** [this was after the Lord's Supper], **they went out to the Mount of Olives.** That's where Jesus was arrested. And Matthew 28:16 says, **Then the eleven disciples went away into Galilee, to the mountain which Jesus had appointed for them.**

I love that Scripture. It's not something you'd memorize in your daily Bible study, but I love it. **The eleven disciples went away...to the mountain which Jesus had appointed for them.**

God has appointed a mountain for you, where you and He are going to get serious, where there's going to be a transformation and a transfiguration of your own life and you will begin to live at a higher level of life.

But let me ask you a few questions.

- Are you willing to go to the mountain which He has appointed for you?

- Are you willing to climb up it, step by step?

- Are you ready to get out of the normalcy of your everyday routine?

- Are you willing to go where you will meet God and find that higher level of life that He has planned for you?

You can't slip in spending time with God at the "half-time" report; you are going to have to make a way. You can't slip it in after you get done with everything else you want to do; you have to make the time for it. You can't just fit God into your little world and say, "Okay, Lord, go ahead and show me Your stuff." You have to go to the mountain He has appointed for you and meet Him. Then you'll be transfigured, you'll be transformed and your vision will be expanded.

When I stood on top of Mount Rainier, I looked from Washington into Oregon and saw Mount Hood. I could even see what's left of Mount St. Helens after it erupted. You see, when you get on a mountain with God, you get a bigger vision for your life—you can see further.

What are you believing God for? Perhaps you're saying, "If only we could pay this month's rent!" But you will see beyond this month when you get on that mountain with God.

What are you looking at? "Oh, I'm just believing to have enough money to retire," you say. Retire? Why don't you look a little further? Why don't you climb a little higher? There is more life out there than you are looking at with your vision.

"Oh, someday I'm going to get a Winnebago." Come on! Climb the mountain, and get a bigger vision. You can have your Winnebago, but I'm just saying that there is a whole lot more than that. You see, as long as you live in the valley, you can't see much. The disciples, for example, went to the mountain which Jesus had appointed for them, and look what happened:

When they saw Him, they worshiped Him; but some doubted.

And Jesus came and spoke to them, saying, "All authority has been given to Me in heaven and on earth.

"Go therefore and make disciples of all the nations, baptizing them in the name of the Father and of the Son and of the Holy Spirit, teaching them to observe all things that I have commanded you; and lo, I am with you always, even to the end of the age."

Matthew 28:17-20

This is the Great Commission—the marching orders of the Church. They were given to the disciples when they met Jesus at the mountain which He had appointed. And He'll give them to you. But He's not going to do it while you are sitting on your couch. He's not going to give them to you while you have the remote control in your hand. He's not going to give them to you when the only muscle in your body you've exercised is your thumb on that remote control.

To get God's marching orders, you're going to have to climb. That means you are going to have to seek, press, reach and go in your spirit. It means you are going to have to take a few steps.

Are you willing to do that? That's when you'll get the word. That's when you'll get your breakthrough message. That's when you'll get the insight that changes your company. That's when you'll get the truth that makes your marriage what you've always wanted it to be. That's when you'll get the understanding to raise your kids and the breakthrough to get them where God wants them to be. It happens when you meet Jesus at the mountain He has appointed for you. We've got to go there because that is where the supernatural takes place!

PERSONAL APPLICATION OF
SUMMIT-CLIMBING TRUTHS

1. The mountaintop I am climbing toward is _____

_____

_____

2. The "mountain" I go to when I want to be alone with the Lord is _____

_____

3. My power source is _____, and I stay connected by _____

_____

_____

_____

4. My life's vision will be expanded as I _____

_____

_____

_____

5. I am leaving the low life and heading toward the high life by _____

_____

CHAPTER THREE

FIVE REQUIREMENTS FOR
CLIMBING YOUR MOUNTAIN

To climb your mountain of destiny successfully requires five things: desire, drive, discipline, diligence and determination.

DESIRE

Having the desire gets you started on your climb up the mountain of God. Psalm 37:4 says, [God] **shall give you the** *desires* **of your heart.** Mark 11:24 KJV says, **What things soever ye desire, when ye pray, believe that you receive them, and ye shall have them.** You have to desire to see from the higher level. You have to desire to get above the cloud level. You have to desire to go beyond what is normal. You have to desire to get out of the low life and rise up to the higher life. It all starts with *desire.*

Someone said to me, "Pastor Treat, when I don't have desire, what should I do?" Desire to find some desire! Find some "want to."

You say, "I don't even want to have the 'want to' to want to!" Then, ask God to give you the want to to have the want to to get the want to!

Start with some kind of desire. I believe by reading this book you have a desire for God and for what God has for you. I believe you have a desire for something in life that you don't have. Otherwise, instead of reading, you would be sitting around doing nothing.

DRIVE

Second, *climbing the mountain of God takes drive.* In Philippians 3:14, Paul said, **I press toward the goal for the prize of the upward call of God in Christ Jesus.** You must have some drive in you.

I wanted to quit about halfway up Mount Rainier. I wanted to sit down. Man, I wanted to give up! But even when it's no longer fun, you find the drive inside you to keep going. You find the drive to press through. Anyone I have ever talked to who has been successful at anything viewed part of what they had to do as not being fun.

Talk to the businessman who has a successful business. He may not have had a lot of fun, but he had the drive inside to keep him going. People say, "Oh, Pastor, it must be fun getting to preach all over the world." There's really only an hour of fun out of every twenty-four hours of traveling. But you have a drive inside.

Is it fun having kids? About one hour out of every twenty-four. And sometimes you skip that hour! But there's a drive inside to love them and raise them up for the glory of God.

If you have no drive in you, you'll spend your life in the lowlands and you'll never find the mountain of God.

DISCIPLINE

Third, *climbing your mountain will take discipline.* In 1 Corinthians 9:27 Paul said, **But I discipline my body and bring it into subjection, lest, when I have preached to others, I myself should become disqualified.**

Incidentally, a *disciple* is "a disciplined one."

Before we climbed Mount Rainier, we had to train and prepare, in effect becoming disciples. We had to learn how to use the ice axe, how to self-arrest and what to do with the ropes. When someone falls, it is not the time to say, "What do I do?" When you are roped up, you are trusting your friend.

At one point, we were hanging off the side of the part of the mountain called "the chute." You're not just walking up the mountain; you are roped up with your teammates. If you slip, you count on your teammates to hold you up. You have to be disciplined.

Do you have the discipline to climb to where God wants you to be? "Well, I was planning on praying, but the alarm didn't go off!" you might say. No, it went off, but you just kept hitting the snooze button. That compromise button! That lie button! That button that enables you to say, "I'm getting up at 6—no, 6:10—no, 6:20...." So you start the day with compromise. The first act of your day is to backslide. Come on! It takes *discipline* to climb your mountain.

DILIGENCE

Fourth, *it takes diligence.* It takes one more step, one more day, one more prayer, one more act of faith, one more act of love, one more tithe, one more offering. It takes diligence! You stay at it. Proverbs 10:4 says, **He who has a slack hand becomes poor, but the hand of the diligent makes rich.**

DETERMINATION

Fifth, *it takes determination.* In 1 Corinthians 2:2 Paul said, **For I determined not to know anything among you except Jesus Christ and Him crucified.** He's saying, *I'm not going to be trapped by the world. I'm not going to be distracted by the world. I'm not going to compromise with the world. I am determined to know nothing but Jesus Christ and Him crucified.*

If you want to climb your mountain to meet God, see the transfiguration and experience the transformation, you are going to have to have desire, drive, discipline, diligence and determination to get there. And when you get there, you will be quick to acknowledge, "It was all worth it!"

PERSONAL APPLICATION OF SUMMIT-CLIMBING TRUTHS

1. My desire to climb to the summit of my destiny is ___

   _____

   _____

   _____

2. My drive for climbing to the summit of my destiny is

   _____

   _____

   _____

   _____

3. The discipline I need to climb to the summit of my destiny comes from _____

   _____

   _____

   _____

4. I am diligent in my climb out of mediocrity to the summit by _____

   _____

_____

_____

5. My determination to reach the summit of my destiny in order to seek God is motivated by _____

_____

_____

_____

My determination to reach the summit of my destiny in

of the grace of God is not and for

PART 2

LETTING GO
OF THE
LOW LIFE

CHAPTER FOUR

LETTING GO OF THE LOWER LIFE TO FIND THE HIGHER LIFE

God wants to meet with us, because when He meets with us personally, powerfully and face to face, change happens in our lives. The brightness of Christ begins to come out of us. The light of God begins to shine through us. Transformation and transfiguration take place in us—literally we change by becoming less like mere humans and more like our Father God. That should be the goal of every Christian—to be transformed into the image of Christ.

So our daily lives are a process of becoming more like Jesus and less like ourselves. This is what change and transformation are all about. But it doesn't just happen because you go to work this week. It doesn't just happen because you show up for church this week. It only happens as you press in to meet with God—as you hunger and thirst after the presence of God.

There are many Christians who have bumped along through life. They may even be good church members. But they have never experienced what God has for them, nor have they ever really seen the change that they wanted in their lives. They have never had the marriage or the business or the ministry that God has for them. They have never gone up to their mountain of transformation so they could become the people God called them to be.

There is something about climbing that speaks of *overcoming*. Climbing speaks of pressing through challenge, playing with pain, so to speak. Using the natural illustration of my climb up Mount Rainier, I can testify that you don't climb a mountain accidentally. You purpose in your heart to do so, you prepare, you make sacrifices and you go for it. And more than once when you are climbing that mountain, you will wish, think or wonder, *Why am I here? Why am I doing this? It would have been easier just to sit at home and watch the baseball game.*

On our climb, as we reached the highest peak, the summit, and stood on the top of Mount Rainier, we acknowledged that it was worth all that we had gone through to get there— the desire, drive, discipline, diligence and determination.

Getting Out of Your Comfort Zone

Most people—I'm talking about the majority of people in our world today—settle for so little in life. They settle for the "lowlands" with God instead of a mountaintop experience. You have to get out of your comfort zone to go to a higher level in life. Transformation can only take place when you get out of your comfort zone and meet with God on a higher level. Change, transfiguration and transformation can only take place when you climb the mountain of the Lord and meet with Him on that higher level.

Many successful people, mayors, entrepreneurs, educators, ministers, businessmen and businesswomen, politicians and other professional people attend Christian Faith Center. None of these people got where they are or are doing what they are doing by seeking what feels good or looks easy and comfortable. They have accomplished what they have because they did what was uncomfortable. They got out of their comfort zone, bit the bullet, took the pain and went for what they thought God had called them to do.

I repeat, transformation can take place only when you get out of your comfort zone.

In Matthew 10, Jesus talks about all of the things God wants to do in our lives and how we can receive them. Verses 38 and 39 sum it up by saying:

"And he who does not take his cross and follow after Me is not worthy of Me. He who finds his life will lose it, and he who loses his life for My sake will find it."

Verse 39 in *The Amplified Bible* says, **Whoever finds his [lower] life will lose [the higher life], and whoever loses his [lower] life on My account will find [the higher life].**

When I first came to the Lord, I was a bit nervous about becoming a Christian because I thought I would miss out on all of the fun—you know, a lot of the good stuff like probation officers, jail cells, courtrooms, car wrecks and hangovers. I didn't have a whole lot to lose, but somehow in my mind I thought that if I became a Christian, I would lose all the "good stuff." I thought all Christians suffer, struggle and are miserable, but when the Lord comes back, they go to heaven, have eternal life and everything is good.

So I had a hard time with the whole decision. But then I began to realize that everything I gave up was coming back to me in multiplied form. The low life that I lost is not comparable to the high life that I found. People who say, "I'm not going to let go of what I have to get what God has," are misinformed. They are unaware of what God has for them. They are hanging on to their low life and refusing to accept the high life. Anybody who stays locked into his comfort zone—his survival mentality, into "my way, my schedule, my free time, don't mess with me, leave me alone; I'll show up on Sunday, but I don't want to get involved"— is missing out on the higher life. Your comfort zone will keep you from the mountain of transformation.

Why don't more people climb their mountains? Because our top priority is to avoid stress, challenge, embarrassment, pain, hardness or anything that would get us out of our comfort zones. With that mentality, we miss what God wants to do in us on the mountain.

What if Peter had said to Jesus, "You know, Lord, we've been pretty busy. Look at my schedule. See all the places I've been the last couple of weeks? Now You want me to climb the mountain again? Can't we just have the meeting right here?"

What if John said, "Lord, come on! We're tired. We preached last night and the night before. We had a board meeting, a staff meeting and now we have to climb the mountain? What are we going up there for? Isn't this good enough right here?"

I could imagine the Lord's saying, "No, it's not. If you want to see My glory, if you want to see Moses and Elijah, if you want to see transfiguration, if you want to see the power and if you want to hear the audible voice of God, you have to get out of the lowland. Out of your comfort zone. Out of what is natural. Out of where the crowd is. Out of what is easy. Go on up to the mountaintop! And when you get up on the mountaintop, then you'll see what I have for you. Then you'll receive what I have for you."

You can't change if you refuse to move out of your comfort zone. You can't have the high life if you refuse to let go of the low life. In other words, if you are going to stay the way you are, you can't be the way God wants you to be. If you want to hang on to the way you are, you can't have the transformation.

We spend so much time defending the way we are and why we are the way we are that we never get to where we could be. Don't hang on to the old attitude that says, "Well, the way I've always thought...." If that is a common phrase for you, crucify it, because you've got to be willing to give up the low life to attain the high life.

REACHING FOR THE HIGHER LIFE

I always think of this illustration of change and transformation: Everyone's seen the "daring young men on the flying trapeze." One of them is prepared to catch the other one. Since they have to make sure they are in sync, they spend a few minutes swinging and getting the right rhythm.

When they are swinging back and forth high in the air, it's not all that exciting to watch. But when one lets go of his trapeze and he's flying through the air, doing his twists and twirls, that's when the show is on!

Likewise, when you let go of your "trapeze" and you're in the midst of transition, when you let go of what you had but you haven't grabbed on to what you're going to have, you're out there in thin air and all you have is hope. All you have is vision. All you have is faith in the One who will catch you—but you have to let go.

Many Christians are swinging and swinging, but they aren't going anywhere because they don't want to let go. "I've always been this way," they say. "My mama was this way." "My daddy was this way." So stay there! Life may be a bore, but at least you're secure.

But when you let go, you're looking for the One who will catch you! Now you're trusting God for that higher level. You are in transformation. You are on your way to something you have never had before. You are going to a higher place where God can do something *in* you. But you have to let go of the low life before you can find your high life.

Your mountain of transformation is any class, activity, service or relationship that causes you to view things differently and to make changes in your normal way of doing things. If you haven't built a relationship with someone who pushes you out of your norms, then you're stuck in your ruts. If you haven't been around people who cause you to pray a little differently, think a little differently, see a little differently and go for something higher, then you have created a life of comfort zones. You are stuck in your low life.

You may say, "Yeah, but my life is better than that of a lot of people." We're not going to compare ourselves to others. Instead, we are looking to our Father, and we are going to meet with Him. We are not trying to outdo each other; we want to meet with God.

The devil's tricked you into saying, "I am doing better than most people if I stay right here." You're not to compare yourself with anyone else, but you are to meet with God. That's what this transformation is all about. If you always avoid what is uncomfortable, you'll never climb your mountain. If life is a quest for what is nice, easy and comfortable, you will never find what God has for you.

PERSONAL APPLICATION OF SUMMIT-CLIMBING TRUTHS

1. I will press toward the goal of being transformed into the image of Jesus Christ by _____

   _____

   _____

   _____

2. My comfort zone has been _____

   I am moving out of my comfort zone and climbing toward a higher level of life by _____

   _____

   _____

   _____

3. The goal of my higher level of life is _____

   _____

   I will achieve it by _____

   _____

   _____

   _____

CHAPTER FIVE

MOSES WENT UP TO GOD

Exodus 19:3 says, **And Moses went *up* to God....** We are always trying to get God to come down to us, and He has. Jesus became as a man in the likeness of sinful flesh and came *down* to Earth to give His life as a ransom for many. He came down to where you are. He loves you where you are. He has reached out to you where you are. He came down to meet with you, but He didn't do that to leave you there. He did that to save you and fill you with His Spirit and then to take you back up to meet with God.

But we've got a social mentality, a Western pop culture that wants to bring everything down. Bring leadership down to our level. Bring what is good down to the norm. And let's cut down any preacher who tries to lift us up. We want to bring everything down. In fact, that's what they said to Jesus on the cross: **"Save Yourself, and come down from the cross!"** (Mark 15:30).

I've had people say to me, "Why don't you get off your high horse?" I'm not on a horse; I'm riding on the wings of the Lord. But the spirit of our society—the spirit of our age—is to bring everything down.

RISING ABOVE THE NORM

Moses went *up* to meet with God. Are you going to go up and see the glory of God? Are you going to go up to the higher level of life? Are you going to go up to receive what God has for you? Are you going to go up to a life that is above average? Are you going to get up out of your comfort zone and see what God can do with you because you hunger for His presence?

Can you imagine what God could do with a man or a woman who is willing to leave everything to meet with Him? Who will go up? Moses went up to God, and the Lord called to him from the mountain, saying:

"Thus you shall say to the house of Jacob, and tell the children of Israel: You have seen what I did to the Egyptians, and how I bore you on eagles' wings and brought you to Myself.

> "Now therefore, if you will indeed obey My
> voice and keep My covenant, then you shall be a
> special treasure to Me above all people...."
>
> **Exodus 19:3-5**

God is trying to get us up above all other people,
Church! He is trying to get us out of the norm and out of
the average.

Many of us grew up saying to our moms, "Well, everybody's doing it." God's trying to get you *above* what everybody is doing!

"Well, everybody's getting the flu," Christians say. But
we're above that. "Everybody's struggling financially," but
we're above that. "Everybody's getting AIDS," but we're above
that. "The world is going to hell," but we're above that—we
are going to heaven.

God lifts us above people and situations. Stop listening
to the reports of the averages and the norms. Start thinking,
*I've come up to the mountain of God, and He has me living
above the norm.*

Exodus 19:6 says, **"And you shall be to Me a kingdom
of priests and a holy nation."** You see, God didn't want
Israel to be one tribe of priests. He wanted a nation of
priests. He doesn't want the Church to be a few excited
people while the rest of the people are just sitting there,

drooling on themselves! He wants a kingdom of priests who are serving Him and living on a higher level, who are excited about the presence of God—a kingdom of priests and a holy nation.

Moses told the elders what the Lord was saying:

> And Moses brought the people out of the camp to meet with God, and they stood at the foot of the mountain. Now Mount Sinai was completely in smoke, because the Lord descended upon it in fire. Its smoke ascended like the smoke of a furnace, and the whole mountain quaked greatly. And when the blast of the trumpet sounded long and became louder and louder, Moses spoke, and God answered him by voice.

> Exodus 19:17-19

Can you imagine being in God's presence, which is that strong?

In our church, we seek the presence of God. Sometimes we fall down and can't move. Sometimes we feel like we can't even breathe, we're so much in the presence of God. Sometimes our knees are weak and we can't even stand up. I've seen people sitting in their chair looking like they're zoned out.

So, we've had various manifestations of the presence and glory of God, but can you imagine being in a place like this? It wasn't a band that played that trumpet. It was the trump of God—long, loud and louder.

Then the Lord came down upon Mount Sinai, on the top of the mountain (Ex. 19:20). Jesus isn't coming to the valley. He's not coming down into your normal, everyday comfort zones. He's asking you to come *up* to the top of the mountain. **And the Lord called Moses to the top of the mountain, and Moses went *up*** (v. 20).

WILL YOU GO UP?

Who will go up? Who will go up to see Jesus transfigured before them? Who will go up to see the glory of God? Who will go up to see what God has for them? Who will go up to hear the Word of the Lord?

> **Now all the people witnessed the thunderings, the lightning flashes, the sound of the trumpet, and the mountains smoking; and when the people saw it, they trembled and stood afar off.**
>
> **Then they said to Moses, "You speak with us, and we will hear; but let not God speak with us, lest we die."**
>
> **Exodus 20:18,19**

Many people want to hear about God. They want to hear about what God said to someone else. They are interested in what God is doing somewhere else. But we want to be the kind of people who hear and see and sense the presence of God personally. The people said to Moses, "You talk to us, but don't let God talk to us, because He is too radical."

We want the preacher to be nice. We want him to make the Christian lifestyle easy. We want the preacher to make us feel good. Some people say, "When God talks to me, it doesn't always feel good, so don't let Him talk to me."

I don't know how many people have said, "We like the music at Christian Faith Center, but we want to go where we are comfortable." When God speaks to you, it's not always comfortable. When God stirs your spirit, it's not just to make you feel good. God is trying to lift you up to a higher level. He is trying to pick you up so you can be the person He created you to be. Those who died in the wilderness never experienced their full potential and never saw the higher life. I refuse to die in the wilderness of compromise. I want to hear what God has to say to me.

MOSES WENT UP

Exodus 24:15-17 says:

Then Moses went up into the mountain, and a cloud covered the mountain.

Now the glory of the Lord rested on Mount Sinai, and the cloud covered it six days. And on the seventh day He called to Moses out of the midst of the cloud.

The sight of the glory of the Lord was like a consuming fire on the top of the mountain in the eyes of the children of Israel.

Can you imagine? Moses waited six days. He's so hungry for God that he is not leaving until he hears from God.

Finally God begins to speak: **So Moses went into the midst of the cloud and went up into the mountain. And Moses was on the mountain forty days and forty nights** (Ex. 24:18). Apparently Moses didn't sleep or eat for forty days and forty nights. In the glory of God, you don't need sleep and you don't need food. The presence of God will sustain you.

While Moses was there, God told him everything about the tabernacle and most of the laws of the old covenant. He imparted all of it into Moses' spirit and soul during the forty days and forty nights. It is possible that this is when God gave Moses the book of Genesis, with Moses writing the creation account, telling us about Adam and Eve and the serpent and all that went on in those early years. In the presence of God, the Word of God for God's people came to Moses.

You and I are not Moses, and we will never lead Israel as Moses did. But in our own lives, if we'll get into God's presence, if we will hunger to meet with God, we will have the Word of the Lord for our families. We will know the will of God for our lives, for our businesses and for our ministries. We won't be like so many people who, after they have been saved for ten, twelve or fifteen years, still don't know what God has called them to do. They are still wandering around, trying to figure out how to get out of debt. They are still trying to figure out if it is God's will to heal them. Come on! Get into relationship with God, and you will know what He wants you to do with your life. God doesn't want you to live your life with doubts and questions.

When Moses got into the presence of God, he knew exactly what God wanted him to do for the rest of his life. I'm not talking about a one-time special event. I am talking about a lifestyle of seeking God—a daily, regular part of our lives.

DEVELOPING YOUR RELATIONSHIP WITH THE LORD

Here's a great story in Exodus 33:15-16 that you need to understand:

> **[Moses] said to Him [God], "If Your Presence does not go with us, do not bring us up from here. For how then will it be known that Your people and I have found grace in Your sight, except You go with us?"**

How are people going to know that you're a Christian? Because you don't smoke? Because you don't drink beer? Because you've got a fish symbol on your bumper or a key chain that says "Jesus"? How will people know?

We've had such religious thinking: *Well, they will know I'm a Christian because I'm a nice person.* There are lots of nice people who don't believe in Jesus. We think, *They will know I'm a Christian because I go to church on Sunday.* A lot of people go to church who don't believe Jesus is Lord.

How do other people know you're a Christian? *God's presence goes with you.* That's what separates you and makes you different.

When everyone else panics, the peace of God that passes understanding guards our hearts and minds. When everyone else is afraid, the faith of God guards our hearts. When everyone else is confused, we have answers. When everyone else is angry, we have joy. When everyone else is upset, we have peace. *It's the peace of God in our lives that separates us from this world.*

And as the world gets darker and darker, with more disease and despair, the presence of God will shine brighter and brighter. Make sure you go up to your mountain to be transfigured, because without God's presence you are no different than anyone else. Come on! It's true!

You say, "But I responded to the altar call. I prayed the sinner's prayer. I know the Romans' road. I went through the new converts class." This isn't about a prayer. It's not about a class. It's not about a creed. It is about a *relationship*. This is about the presence of the Lord in your life, which is much bigger than a religious routine.

In Exodus 33:17, it says, **The Lord said to Moses, "I will also do this thing that you have spoken; for you have found grace in My sight, and I know you by name."** Can you imagine God's doing something because a man asks Him to? I love that! God does the very things His people ask Him to do.

"I'll do this thing because I like you, Moses, and I know you by name."

Moses says, "I'm on a roll, so I'm going to ask for more! Seems like I found God in a good mood. Let's see what else we can get going today!"

Look at verse 18: **And he [Moses] said, "Please, show me Your glory."** Moses is being bold! While the average person worries about what's for dinner, Moses is hungry for the glory of God. While the average person is squabbling over who squeezed the toothpaste the wrong way, Moses is hungry for the glory of God. While the average person is arguing over who slammed the door and who left the light on, Moses is hungry for the glory of God. While the average person is looking for someone to make him feel good, Moses is saying, "God, just one more thing. May I see Your glory?"

In verses 19-23 God answers Moses' question:

"I will make all My goodness pass before you, and I will proclaim the name of the Lord before you. I will be gracious to whom I will be gracious, and I will have compassion on whom I will have compassion."

But He said, "You cannot see My face; for no man shall see Me, and live."

And the Lord said, "Here is a place by Me, and you shall stand on the rock. So it shall be, while My glory passes by, that I will put you in the cleft of the rock, and will cover you with My hand while I pass by. Then I will take away My hand, and you shall see My back; but My face shall not be seen."

More than just experiencing what Moses went through, I want to have my own contact with God. I want to have my own relationship and experience. This isn't about creeds and doctrines. *This is about God's presence in our lives.*

What is climbing the mountain of transfiguration all about? It's about getting into the presence of God yourself, whether that happens in your bedroom, office, living room, basement or backyard. It must happen if you are going to go where God wants you to go. You've got to have more than a sermon and a cassette tape. You've got to have *the touch of God* on your life.

If we are going to raise up kids who obey God, it's got to be with more than a Sunday school class and a green flannel board. Our children must recognize, "God is in our home, God is in our lives and when my dad says something, God does it. When my mom prophesies, it happens. Don't mess with my mom and dad when they are talking to God!"

If you want your kids to obey God, it's not about controlling them and demanding from them. It's about showing them the presence of God and letting them experience His presence.

If we had the heart of Moses, we would say, "Lord, today I'm not so concerned with where I live, what I eat, how I dress or all the things of this world. But this one thing I'd like to talk with You about. Could You just show me Your glory? Could You reveal a little more of Yourself to me? Could You bring a little more of Your presence into my life?"

If we hunger and thirst after the presence of God, He will show Himself to us. He will meet us. That means we are moving out of our comfort zones. We are climbing up to that higher place. Moses got away from the people who weren't hungry for God and who didn't even want to hear His voice. He went to that higher place. Others would not go with him.

Most people won't go with you either, but your hunger for God is what matters. Those who never go to the mountain—who never see the glory and never hear the voice of the Lord—will settle for a man-made religion.

When Moses was on the mountain for forty days and forty nights, the Israelites made their own god—a golden calf. So when Moses came down from the mountain and saw it, he was a little ticked off. I mean, he burned the golden calf, ground it to powder, scattered it on the water and made the Israelites literally drink the god they had made! (Ex. 32:20.)

But you don't have to be like the disobedient Israelites, who settled for the low life and man-made religion; you can be like Moses, who asked God for one thing: more of His presence!

PERSONAL APPLICATION OF SUMMIT-CLIMBING TRUTHS

1. I will rise up above what the world calls average by

   _____

   _____

   _____

   _____

2. I don't want to simply hear *about* God; I want to "go up," as Moses did, to experience His presence personally, because _____

   _____

   _____

   _____

3. The "wilderness of compromise" is not for me because

   _____

   _____

   _____

4. The greatest change I expect to experience in the presence of God's glory is _____

   _____

PART 3

CLIMBING YOUR DESTINY MOUNTAIN

CHAPTER SIX

CLIMBING TO A HIGHER SPIRITUAL PLANE

Matthew 17:1-2 says:

Now after six days Jesus took Peter, James, and John his brother, led them up on a high mountain by themselves; and He was transfigured before them. His face shone like the sun, and His clothes became as white as the light.

Everyone wants to see Jesus in one way or another. Many of us don't really know what that means, but we have a desire to know God, to see the reality and the truth of God. The world is crying out for the reality and the truth of God. They want to see something spiritual and powerful. They are making programs about aliens, angels, spirits, forces and every imaginary thing, because they are looking for something real. They are looking for reality, because they know there is more beyond this physical, natural world.

Very few people want to go up on the mountain of God by themselves. They want to stay down in their sin. They want to stay down in their own compromises. They want to stay down in their own circumstances—yet they want to see God.

Jesus took Peter, James and John up on a high mountain by themselves. They got away from the crowd. They got away from the average. They got away from the norm. They got away from "the way everybody does it." They went to a higher level of life—a higher level of righteousness, integrity, honesty and desire. And that's where they saw Jesus transfigured before them. That's where they saw the glory. That's where they saw the light and where they heard the voice of God saying to Jesus, **"You are My beloved Son; in You I am well pleased"** (Luke 3:22).

God wants to transform and transfigure your life with His light and His glory. He wants to meet with you. He wants to show Himself to you. God wants to bring you to that place where *you* see Him in a real, personal, intimate, powerful way.

But it's not going to happen while you are watching TV or checking on the latest score of the game. It's not going to happen in the low life. It's going to happen when you seek God on the mountain. I am talking about climbing to a higher spiritual plane. I'm talking about moving up to a greater faith, a greater desire, a greater commitment in your relationship with God.

I am not talking about trying to fit God into *your* program; I'm talking about you fitting into His program. I am not talking about just going to church when it is easy, comfortable and the church does things you like. I am talking about going through the pain and discomfort of climbing to that higher level of life in Christ. It's there for all of us. Those who will go for it are going to find exciting transformation, change, fulfillment and a life that the average person never finds.

But if you are hanging on to your low life—defending the way you are, defending your schedule, fighting for your own free time, trying to stay away from commitments, challenges and changes, hanging on to the way you want things to be and the way they have always been—you will lose the high life. You will never climb to a higher spiritual plane.

On the other hand, when you are willing to lose the low life, you will say, "I'm not defending the way I've thought. I'm not defending the way I've lived. I'm not hanging on to the way I've done things. But I am seeking for something higher. I am giving up what I have had so I can have something new. I am letting go of the way it has been so I can have something different. I am losing my low life because I am going to find a higher level of life." When you have that kind of spirit, you are ready to climb!

MOVING UP HIGHER!

When eight of us climbed Mount Rainier—one of the highest peaks in the continental United States—we climbed up to the summit, the very peak of Mount Rainier, which is just under 15,000 feet. In that climb, we went through all kinds of changes. We'd gone through seven months of preparation, pain and commitment. And there were times when the climb wasn't all that much fun! With forty pounds on your back and slogging through the snow, I began to say to some of the folks around me, "This isn't fun. I'm tired and hurting already." We all started making jokes about it because we all felt the same way. We were going through the same difficulties.

I thought, *You know what? There is somebody at home in Seattle right now sitting on their couch, resting, having a double latte, and I'm here on this mountain, hurting, with forty pounds on my back. It's not fun!*

But I turned around when we were at about 10,000 feet and looked over at the summit of Mount St. Helens. I looked over at the summit of Mount Adams and beyond that down to Mount Hood in Oregon. I could see for miles and miles and miles.

Then I looked up to the summit of Mount Rainier, which almost seemed touchable, and thought, *You know, sitting on my couch and adding inches to my behind, I can't have this view. I can't have this experience. I can't see this vision.*

See, there's an easy way. There's a comfortable way. There's a normal way. But you cannot experience all this world has to offer and all that God has to offer until you stop fighting for your free time, for your comfort, for the way you've always had it and the way you've always wanted it. It's time to lose the low life and start reaching for something higher.

Of course our trek to the summit of Mount Rainier was a natural, physical thing, which in itself had little spiritual benefit. But when you apply it to your attitude and to your spiritual life—when you lose your way and find God's way—you rise to a much higher level of life.

I spent so many years trying to get high, and instead I just got lower and lower. But one day I ran right into the most high God! And when I gave up that old way, I found a new way. I gave up the low life and I found a high life.

Let's press on to the higher life!

DILIGENCE WILL MOVE YOU HIGHER

I gave you some "D" requirements for climbing your mountain: *desire, drive, discipline, diligence and determination.* The one word that keeps coming back to me and sticking out to me is *diligence.* You will prosper when you are diligent, not when the welfare system kicks in, not when the union steps up, not when you are lucky, not when your lottery ticket wins. The hand of the *diligent* will make you rich. (Prov. 10:4.)

I have always thought of diligence as hanging in there and sticking to it. But you can stick to mediocrity, and after thirty years of sticking to it, you've got a mediocre life. You can stick to a sluggardly attitude, and after thirty years of having that kind of attitude, you've got a sluggard's life! You may be a stick-to-it person, but the thing you are sticking to may not get you any higher. You are sticking to the low life. You are hanging in there with your old attitudes. You are being faithful in your mediocrity. You've got to be diligent. The word *diligent* in Hebrew is *charuwts* or *charuts,* which means "to be incisive, to cut away everything that's not important."[1]

The words *incisive* and *decisive* literally come from a word that means, "a sharp threshing or cutting instrument having sharp teeth."[2]

You may say, "What does that have to do with diligence?"

A diligent person isn't someone who goes through the routine of everyday life, functioning on a low level. They may be consistent, yes, and maybe that is to be admired. But when you just do the same old thing every day and you keep getting the same old results, you begin to realize, "Wait a minute. I've got to lose the low life so I can find the high life."

In the Hebrew, *decisive* literally means "dredging or trenching out and mining gold."[3]

The diligent person starts cutting through the surface, moving beyond the norm. He or she starts getting the real results and benefits of the "gold" of life. The hand of the diligent will make you rich.

"Well, Brother Treat, I've gone to work every day for twenty-seven years, and I haven't missed a day yet."

Well, twenty-seven years at $5 an hour isn't going to get you very far. The diligent cut through the low life and move on to the deeper and higher life. They press where they can really begin to produce results.

Proverbs 12:24 says, **The hand of the diligent will rule, but the lazy man will be put to forced labor.** Proverbs 13:4 says, **The soul of a lazy man desires, and has nothing; but the soul of the diligent shall be made rich.** Proverbs 21:5

says, **The plans of the diligent lead surely to plenty, but those of everyone who is hasty** [and buys lottery tickets!], **surely to poverty.** Proverbs 22:29 KJV says, **Seest thou a man diligent in his business? he shall stand before kings; he shall not stand before mean men.** Proverbs 27:23 KJV says, **Be thou diligent to know the state of thy flocks, and look well to thy herds.**

God is trying to lift us higher. He is telling us, "Here's what it takes to climb to a higher life. Here's how you get to the abundance. Here's where you go to find the blessings I have provided for you." God doesn't want us to settle for less than His perfect will. He doesn't want us to survive and barely get by. He is moving us up the mountain to a higher life. There is more than you have ever experienced. It's just a matter of learning how to climb the mountain of God to get it.

A SPECTATOR'S MENTALITY WILL KEEP YOU DOWN

We are going to cut through the waste, the superfluous, and get to those things that produce results in our lives, that help us rise up in life, that keep us moving forward. We are not going to settle just for survival—making a living and getting by. We don't want a marriage that just gets by;

we want a marriage that's fun. We don't want kids that just go out and get jobs. We want to raise up kids who have generational blessings on their lives and who will fulfill their destinies.

At the end of our lives, we won't have to say, "Well, I paid the bills." Instead, we'll be able to say, "I fulfilled the will of God." That's life on a higher plane.

Remember what they said after Moses had been on the mountain and experienced the glory of God? He went up to get the Word of God where the glory cloud covered the mountain. Exodus 24:17 says, **The sight of the glory of the Lord was like a consuming fire on the top of the mountain in the eyes of the children of Israel.** The people said to Moses after he had been up there forty days and forty nights, "You tell us what God said, but we don't want to meet Him face to face." (Ex. 20:19.)

Our society is much like Israel. We want to see someone else do it. We don't want to do it ourselves. We'd rather watch baseball than play baseball. We'd rather watch football than play football. We'd rather watch golf than play golf. We'd rather watch church than play church. Now, I don't mean "play" in the sense of making it a game; I mean it in the sense of being a part.

We'd rather hear about someone else who heard from God than spend the time on the mountain to hear from God ourselves. Come on! We'd rather go to a concert than a prayer meeting. We'd rather go to a show than have an experience with God. We want a church that lets us sit in our pew but doesn't make us do anything besides that.

Many of us have a spectator's mentality, just like Israel had. We say, "You go talk to God and come back and tell us what He said, We don't want to talk to Him personally," Why? I'm convinced we do because many of us have been tricked by the devil, and we believe we just can't draw close to God ourselves. We believe we can't handle it. We are convinced that we are not able, so we have to watch somebody else. We are convinced that we're no good, so we've got to watch somebody else. We are convinced we don't have the time or the talent, we're not spiritual enough or something is wrong with us or lacking in us, so we watch someone else. We've become a nation of spectators.

Even if we come up with a new medicine, we get sicker. Regardless of the number of new diet programs, we get heavier. It doesn't matter how many new exercise machines come out, we get bigger, because we are a nation that's watching but not experiencing.

So what happens in the Church? We hear about miracles that used to be, but we never experience a miracle.

We hear about blessings that others received, but we never receive them. We hear about the preacher who saw and heard and went and did, but we never see or hear or go or do. We've become a nation of spectators, just like Israel. "You go up there," we say, "and then come back and tell us what it's like." Somehow we have excluded ourselves from the experience.

GET OUT OF THE BLEACHERS AND GET INTO THE GAME!

I have a desire for you to be someone who not only hears about the great things God has done, but you get right into the middle of what God is doing. That may be different for you because you've only watched the game but you've never played it. Or you sat on the couch while someone else climbed the mountain.

That's what it's all about—doing something different, losing the old way so you can find the new way, losing the low life so you can move to the high life, letting go of what you had so you can have what you want. That's the kind of people we are.

Why do we tend to exclude ourselves from doing what we really want to do? We don't believe we have what it takes. I don't know how many people have said to me since I was up on the summit of Mount Rainier, "Oh, I've always wanted to be there, but I could never do that."

Why? "I don't have the time," or "I'm not strong," or "I'm not trained. I don't have experience." We all have something we could allow to exclude us from the higher life. Or there is something we're missing that keeps us from reaching that place where God is pouring out His abundance. You may think you don't have time. You're too old. You're too young. It's your husband. Your wife. Your kids. Past failures. Something causes you to think, *I just don't think I'll ever be that kind of person. I don't think I'll ever have that experience. I don't have what it takes.*

I came to myself a few months before we climbed the mountain. I said, "I've been looking at that thing ever since my grandfather drove me around it, we camped on it and we looked at it from every angle." Finally I said, "I'm going to climb that dude. I'm forty-two years old, so I might as well do it now. It isn't getting any smaller, and I'm not getting any stronger. I might as well just do it."

We started our preparation—gathering equipment, learning how to pack the backpack, learning what equipment we needed to function at an altitude where the air is thinner and how to eat and sleep on the mountain. After going through all that process, we finally started. In the first few hours, I was hurting and tired. There was no fanfare, no congregation to shout, "Yea! He's doing it!" There was nobody saying, "Go, man, go! You can make it!"

On the first day I began to think, *I'm not going to make it. I don't think I want to make it to the summit.* The second day I was convinced, *I am not going to make it! There's just no way! This mountain is too big, and I am tired. Besides, who cares? I mean, I won't get a plaque for this! I won't get paid for doing it. Why am I doing it? It must have been the devil who told me to do this!*

I was going through all this in my mind. But many of us are hurting and tired. And the only reason I didn't stop was that I didn't want to be by myself! Everybody else kept going, so I kept going.

But the third day, suddenly I felt good. If I was hurting, I wasn't thinking about it as much. I had worked through it and overcome it, and the pack didn't seem as heavy as it had the first two days. The air didn't seem as thin as it was the day before either. And by then I could see the summit.

By the third day, there was no doubt in my mind: *I'm going to the top! I'm going to stand on top of this mountain. Then, every day for the rest of my life, when I look at Mount Rainier, I'm going to say, "I stood on top of you!"*

Here's what I'm trying to get across to you. Once you get going, you find strength you didn't know you had, ability you didn't know was there and the "whatever it takes" attitude you didn't think you had. You will have all those things when you need them.

Where does a woman get the strength to give birth to an eight-, nine- or ten-pound baby? She didn't have the strength until she needed it. There have been some nice, sweet, frail women who turned into tigers when they needed strength in childbirth. When you need it, suddenly you have it.

Perhaps you haven't started the college course that you need for your business, your career or your future because you don't think you have what it takes to complete it. But if you will go after it, you will find what it takes to learn what you need to go to a higher level. Or maybe you haven't gotten your college degree because the enemy has convinced you: *You're too slow in your reading and too dumb in your study habits. You'll never be able to complete school.*

That may be true in the natural, but if you will begin to go after it, you will find whatever you need to complete your degree and go on to the next level in your life. Maybe you haven't stepped out in your business or "birthed" that entrepreneurial venture because you are afraid you don't have what it takes. Even though that may be true in the natural, when you reach that goal, you will find out that you do have what it takes. God is working in you. He is on your side. He is trying to get you up to that higher level. Do what it takes!

In Philippians 2:13, God says something very powerful: **For it is God who works in you both to will and to do for His good pleasure.** The word *work* in the Greek is *energeo* from which we get the word *energy*. It means "to be effectually at work, doing things that produce results or to make something happen." God effectually works in you. The word *energeo* connotes energy, strength and power.[4]

The women I mentioned before didn't need the energy, strength or power to give birth to their babies until it was time for delivery. When it's time to deliver that baby, you will have what you need to make it happen.

"I don't think I can climb that mountain," you may say. You don't think you can because you're sitting down in the lowlands. "I don't think I can carry that pack." You don't need to, because you're just trying to get your behind out of your car! But you can get up there on that mountain, and you can do it! You can find a way. You will have the energy, strength and power because God is working in you.

Or you might say, "I don't think I can get through that college course." You can't because you're sitting around, watching TV every night. But get signed up for the course, show up for class, get your books out and ask God to help you.

Suddenly, you'll find you can read more quickly than you thought you could. You can hear and understand better than you thought you could. You can remember more than you thought you could. You'll go through the course and receive your degree, and you'll say, "I did it!"

When you get where you need to be, the energy of God—God working in you—will be there.

Or you might say, "I don't think I can create a company. I don't think I can be an entrepreneur. I don't think I can be my own boss." No, you can't because you're just showing up to pump gas at the local gas station. But you'll get it if you step out in that entrepreneurial venture, take the next step and go to that higher level. Suddenly God will work in you! His energy, strength and power will start flowing in you. You'll have what it takes!

You don't have it when you don't need it. But when you need it, you'll have what it takes. Philippians 2:13 in *The Amplified Bible* says, **[Not in your own strength]** [I love that!] **for it is God who is all the while effectually at work in you—[energizing and creating in you the power and desire]—both to will and to work for His good pleasure and satisfaction and delight.**

Your climb to a higher spiritual plane begins with a desire. How did I end up at the top of Mount Rainier? One day while looking at that mountain I said, "I want to stand on top of it."

How did Christian Faith Center begin? One day in prayer God gave me the desire to have a church in South Seattle that makes a difference in this part of the world and spreads out all over the world.

How does a marriage start? You see a woman and you have a desire to marry her. You see a man and you have a desire to marry him. Everything God does starts with a *desire.*

What happens when you first start living this higher life? You start having desires that you've never had before. In fact, usually it starts through dissatisfaction. You thought everything was cool until you started reading the Bible and found out what God really had for you.

Suddenly you're saying, "Wait a minute, this marriage is a joke. We're not really loving each other. We're just putting up with each other. We're not celebrating our marriage. We're just trying to avoid a crisis." All of a sudden, there is dissatisfaction.

You're saying, "Before I started going to church, everything was pretty good. Since I started going, I realize my life is a wreck!" That creates a desire for the higher life in your marriage, in your career, in your ministry, in your relationships and in every area of your life.

PERSONAL APPLICATION OF SUMMIT-CLIMBING TRUTHS

1. Instead of fitting God into my program, I am getting into His program for me by _____

   _____

   _____

   _____

2. I am reaching for the higher life by _____

   _____

   _____

   _____

3. I am diligent in pursuing God's destiny for my life, which is _____

   _____

   _____

   _____

4. The consuming fire of the glory of the Lord will affect me by _____

   _____

5. I'll get right in the middle of what God is doing by

_____

_____

_____

_____

CHAPTER SEVEN

NO ROOM FOR COMPROMISE

And seeing the multitudes, He went *up* on a mountain... (Matt. 5:1). Jesus continues to go up on the mountain. Look what happens next: **When He was seated His disciples came to Him.**

So often we want God to come down to us, which He has done. He has come down to our pain, down to our problems and down to our conditions. But now God is saying, "It's time for you to come up to Me. Come up to My blessing. Come up to healing. Come up to prosperity. Come up to peace. Come up to joy. Stop living down!"

It's time for you to climb the mountain of transfiguration, climb up that mountain where you can meet God and begin to receive what He has for you. Take one more step. Be diligent. Keep going. Don't stop. Don't quit. Go all the way to the top.

Years ago, when Christian Faith Center was started, people said we wouldn't last long. They said, "It's just a flash in the pan. He's a young, red-headed whippersnapper. That church will go away in a hurry. We've seen them come, and we've seen them go."

But after five years they said, "He's still going." After ten years they said, "He's still going." After fifteen and twenty years they said, "He's still going." After twenty-five years, after fifty years, even after seventy-five years, they will continue to say, "They are still going!" Christian Faith Center and Dominion College will still be going. I'll be seen in a little founder's picture on a wall somewhere, but we'll still be going. Why? Because we are climbing up to God. We are not giving excuses for living in the valley. We're not settling for life in the lowlands. We're not hanging around in debt, poverty, depression and discouragement. We're going up the mountain to meet God and be in His presence, His blessings and His power.

Moses received the Word of God. He was in a cloud of glory for forty days and forty nights, and God was dealing with him. But remember what the people said to Moses? **You speak with us, and we will hear; but let not God speak with us, lest we die** (Ex. 20:19).

When you do not want to climb that mountain, when you don't want to get into the presence of God, when you don't want to go to church and pray and worship and let God inhabit your praise, when you don't want to take time during your week to seek God, when you don't want to hear from God personally, then something else will take the place of God in your life. When you don't want to talk to God for yourself, something else will slowly creep into your life and take the place of God's Word, His voice and His presence.

Look what happened to Israel in Exodus 32:1:

> **Now when the people saw that Moses delayed coming down from the mountain, the people gathered together to Aaron, and said to him, "Come, make us gods that shall go before us; for as for this Moses, the man who brought us up out of the land of Egypt, we do not know what has become of him."**

Moses was only gone for forty days, and the Israelites came to the conclusion that they should make their own god.

After a month of missing church services, of not praying regularly, of not giving and not plugging into the Word of God, people start making a new god—their own god.

> **And Aaron said to them, "Break off the golden earrings, which are in the ears of your wives, your sons, and your daughters, and bring them to me"** (Ex. 32:2).

There is always a leader who will do what the people want, as opposed to what God wants. If you want a leader who will give you what you want—not what God wants—

there's always an Aaron to be found. Moses was *up* hearing from God, while Aaron was *down* listening to the people.

So all the people broke off the golden earrings which were in their ears, and brought them to Aaron.

And he received the gold from their hand, and he fashioned it with an engraving tool, and made a molded calf. Then they said, "This is your god, O Israel, that brought you out of the land of Egypt!"

Exodus 32:3,4

What a slap in God's face! They made a golden calf and claimed that was the god who'd brought them out of Egypt. We're talking about people who had been in slavery for 430 years—who had seen God send ten plagues to deliver them out of Egypt, who had seen God take the wealth of the world and put it into their hands when they left, who had seen God as a pillar of fire by night and a pillar of cloud by day. They had seen the God who split the Red Sea so they could walk over on dry ground, the God who then rolled back the water and drowned the whole Egyptian army. We're talking about a God of miracles!

The Israelites made a silly golden calf and said it was the one who delivered them. You see, when you don't climb the mountain of God, you make your own god, and it's always something demeaning. Some men make a god out of pornography. Others make gods out of their cars or their fishing poles or their golf games. Once I even saw a T-shirt that said, "In Golf I Trust." I didn't know whether to laugh at the man wearing it or to slap him. I thought of the calf, and thought, *This is your god.*

You say, "I would never do that, brother." Wait a minute! How many times have you or someone you know said, "I don't have time for church"?

"What are you doing?"

"Going fishing."

Or, "It's hunting season, bless God, and I'm going hunting."

You're out there looking for Bambi! You've got money to spend on everything you want. You've got time to do whatever you want. But you allow no time for God.

The Israelites made a god of a calf. Some women make gods of their homes. You've got time for everything you want to do. You study interior decorating books, you know the right furniture stores, you've been to all the designer places, but you don't have time to read the Word. You're more committed to your furniture than you are to God.

It is easy for any of us to make a golden calf. It starts by taking our focus, our finances and our energy off God. Anytime something becomes more important than your walk with God, you've got yourself a golden calf.

God said to Moses, "Get down because your people have messed up." Whenever God says, "They're *your* people," you know He's not happy. Moses came down from the mountain and the presence of God with the two tablets of stone—the Ten Commandments. He has been in the glory cloud on the mountain of God.

But when he came down and saw the Israelites dancing and celebrating around the golden calf, **he cast the tablets out of his hands and broke them at the foot of the mountain** (Ex. 32:19). He broke the stone tablets that God made, and he began to prophesy over the people. Thousands of them died that day because of their disobedience. (Ex. 32:26-28.)

Moses was passionate because he loved these people. He would have given his life for them. God showed up and said:

> **"Let Me alone, that My wrath may burn hot against them and I may consume them. And I will make of you a great nation."**
>
> **Then Moses pleaded with the Lord his God, and said: "Lord, why does Your wrath burn hot against Your people whom You have brought out of the land of Egypt with great power and with a mighty hand? Why should the Egyptians speak, and say, 'He brought them out to harm them, to kill them in**

the mountains, and to consume them from the face of the earth'? Turn from Your fierce wrath, and relent from this harm to Your people." [Moses was really saying, "God, check Your attitude!"]

Exodus 32:10-12

I'm telling you, Moses loved those folks! To stand in front of God and say, "Lord, change Your plan, Your thinking, and relent from the fierceness of Your wrath," you've got to have some kind of passion for the people.

There were a couple of other times when Moses wanted to kill them all. He was mad and upset, and God said, "It's okay, Moses, we'll make it through this together." (That's my translation!)

It's a good thing God and Moses never got into agreement on the wrath thing! God would have said, "I'm going to consume them," and Moses would have said, "Go ahead!" I mean, it would have been over. Israel would have been history!

Although Moses had such passion, he still prophesied judgment, and thousands died. He was mad and upset. Why? When you love people, several things happen:

- You hate to see them settle for anything less than God's best.

- You don't want them living in the lowlands. You want to take them to the mountaintop.

- It upsets you to see them in debt when you know God wants them to prosper.

- It hurts you to see them sick when you know God wants them well.

- It upsets you to see them down when God wants them up.

- It upsets you to see them compromise the promises of God.

DON'T QUIT NOW!

As I've already shared, when I was climbing Mount Rainier, I was ready to compromise and say, "I've gone far enough," because my feet hurt, my body hurt, my head hurt—everything hurt! I could have said, "I'm a pastor, not a mountaineer. Just coming this far, that's good enough. I'm about halfway up. I could say I went halfway up. How many people even make it that far? I think I'll just stop right here."

Some leaders from our church—three men who are mountaineers—were with us. They were a real help to me. One of these men came over to me when we were taking a break and said, "Casey, you're not thinking about stopping, are you?"

I said, "Well, I-I-I don't know if I can make it."

He said, "No, no, you're doing great. You're doing good. You've got it made."

He said, "I've brought people up here who were in so much worse shape than you. You're going to make it. No problem!"

That caused me to go one more day. The next day I'm thinking, *I'm not going to make it. I don't have what it takes. I'm not able.*

One of the people on the team had gotten altitude sickness and was throwing up. I was concerned for her as well as for myself, but the leader came to me and said, "No problem. It happens all the time. You're going to the top. All of us are going to the top—no option, no compromise! We can do it! We can make it! If you quit now, you'll be so upset with yourself. We're going to the top. Besides, you don't know the way back, and I won't show you if you quit now!"

I said, "Okay, let's keep going. No option." On the third day, suddenly it hit me, "I can do this. In my spirit I'm already at the top. I've got to get my body to follow now. I've made it. I've done it. I've accomplished it."

Sometimes you have to have someone with you who won't let you stop or quit. You've got to have a Moses who says, "No, you're not going to die in this wilderness. No, you're not going to settle for some calf god. We're going for the high life. We're going for the best."

Sometimes other people believe in you more than you believe in yourself! Thank God that man believed in me, or I would be frustrated today. I'd be saying, "Well, I went halfway!" What kind of testimony is that?

Now I look at Mount Rainier and say, "You see the highest point—the very tip of the summit? I stood on that dude. I stood on the top of that thing." One big reason I made it was that I had a leader who wouldn't let me stop halfway up.

In our Christian walk, Jesus is that leader.

When I first got saved, I didn't think I could live the Christian life. But a sixty-four-year-old black man named Julius Young said, "Big Red,"—that's what he called me—"you're going to live this life. You're not only going to be a good Christian, but you're going to be a Christian leader."

There are times when others believe in you more than you believe in yourself, and they won't let you stop until you get to the top!

For those who hang around me or my pastors, leaders, board members or regents, we are going to carry you to the top. We are going to drag you to the top. We are going to preach you to the top. We are going to prophesy you to the top. We are going to get you up that mountain one way or another. We don't want you to settle for halfway. We don't want to leave you sick halfway up your mountain.

There is a promised land for you—a land of abundance for you, a place of prosperity for you, a place of blessing for you, a good marriage for you, peace and joy for you. There's more for you than you could ask or think, and I don't want you to stop until you get it. I don't want you to give up on yourself and accept a compromise. A compromise is really when you take what you don't want because you won't fight for what you really want. It's accepting less because you are tired of fighting for the real thing.

Don't compromise! Go for the real promise!

PERSONAL APPLICATION OF SUMMIT-CLIMBING TRUTHS

1. Areas of compromise which I need to replace with a
   fervency for God are _____

   _____

   _____

2. I'll not compromise, but I will hold out for God's best
   by _____

   _____

   _____

3. I have someone to encourage me when I feel like giving
   up or quitting. That person is _____

4. My promised land is _____

   _____

   _____

   _____

Chapter Eight

Roping Up in Right Relationships

If you want to see the glory of God, the real expression of God's will, plan and purpose for your life, if you want to see the highest level of life, you've got to get up! You can't live down in yourself, in your fears, in your circumstances, in your limitations or in your attitudes. Get up so God can begin to show Himself strong in your life.

There is one problem about climbing a mountain: It's not easy! We don't like things that aren't easy. Climbing gets tiring, and we don't like getting tired. Climbing takes diligence and effort, and most of us settle for less than God's best because we don't want to put in the effort. We don't want to take the step to get to that next level. I'm telling you, it's worth it. You can do it. You are going to make it!

As a pastor, one of the worst things I see is people who never rise up with God and never rise up with God's vision, plan and purpose for their lives. They just live a low life. What a bummer!

As we were climbing Mount Rainier, when we got up to around 9,000 or 10,000 feet, we were tired and ached all over. The thought came to me, *Maybe we should camp right here. We're more than halfway up the mountain. This is pretty good!*

Some people never start climbing because they settle for "okay." Some stop about halfway up because they settle for "pretty good." "I've done something," they say. "I'm above average. I've made a little progress."

I know I never would have been satisfied if I hadn't gone to the summit—symbolically to God's perfect will, to the highest life, to the most complete destiny and plan that He had for me.

Let's not settle for pretty good. Let's not settle for not bad. Let's go to the summit. That means we've got to make the extra effort to keep on going.

You Can't Go Alone!

There were some things we needed in order to climb Mount Rainier. One was a big rope. If you're not able to rope up with your team, you won't make it to the summit. The number-one lesson for any major climb—and this is so true in your spiritual life as well—is that *you simply cannot make it to the summit by yourself*. You can't go alone. It's nearly impossible. By yourself you might die, get lost or get hurt.

When you get to a certain place on the mountain, you have to rope up. So you get your ropes out and get your team set. A teammate takes the front of the rope, puts it on his harness and hooks it together with the rope on another person's harness. All the teammates hook up together. Once everyone is harnessed together, you head up the mountain. The reason for this is that if someone falls, his partner is there to hold him steady.

In a similar manner, you cannot make it through the affairs of life alone without stumbling now and then. That's normal. But when you're climbing, struggling or fighting alone and you stumble, you self-arrest. In other words, you anchor yourself on that mountain.

That's why we had an ice axe. Now, I'd always thought people carried ice axes to look cool! I'd thought they carried them to scare people or to chip off a little ice if they got thirsty. But no, the ice axe is a life-saving tool you must have for mountain climbing. If someone stumbles before you're roped up, you learn to hit the snow and jam the ice axe in to hold you on the side of the mountain.

We had been doing the right things, working together and following the plan. We were walking along when Steve, the one leading the way, stepped on the edge of a crevasse, and it broke off.

When Steve fell off into the crevasse, the rope between us pulled taut, but we knew what to do. We had the right relationship because we were following our teaching. So we hit the ground and self-arrested. Steve was hanging over the edge, but we were solid. (The week after our climb to the summit of Mount Rainier, two people actually died because they didn't follow the "relationship guidelines" and so had no one to catch them when they fell.)

What do you do when you're going through life and you and your spouse get into a crisis and can't seem to solve the arguing and squabbling? What do you do when you keep trying to get your finances in balance and keep going over your budget and you still can't get an answer? You call your friend. You are not alone. You have relationships with people who will dig in and hang on. They keep you from falling into the crevasses in your daily life.

A minister called me and said, "Casey, I'm embarrassed. I don't even want to talk about it, but I've got to talk to somebody. I'm afraid to talk to some people because they would gossip about me. I've got to talk to somebody because

I don't know what to do. My wife and I are in a crisis. We're talking about separating."

I said, "Hey, man, it's okay. We'll self-arrest. Hit the snow! Hang on!"

Then I explained, "Brother, you've slipped into a crevasse, but don't worry—I won't let you fall."

That's the value of right relationships. That's why we build relationships. We don't come to church just to sing songs and go through the service. We have to build relationships together.

Building Relationships

Some people have said, "It doesn't matter if I go to church or not; I'll just get the tape."

Well, when we all go to heaven, we'll send you a video! Come on, give me a break! This is not about tapes and videos—it's about relationships. Get next to each other, take hands, worship God together, have lunch together and share with each other.

Build relationships. Go to a restaurant, sit in a coffee shop, come to dinner at our house. We know that when you fall into a crevasse in life without a rope, you're going to wish you had made time to build relationships.

We have teenagers getting together with my wife, Wendy, to build godly relationships.

We have women getting together on Wednesday mornings to build relationships. I believe every woman who gets together with other women is better because of it. Over the years I've watched great mothers, strong women, leaders, teachers and wives become stronger through building godly relationships.

Some of the men don't participate in our men's ministry. They are mowing the grass, working overtime or cleaning their guns. Come on, man. Do that *after* you have roped up in relationships with the right people!

CLIMBING WITH PEOPLE OF LIKE VISION

When you're on the mountain, if one person is moving slowly, everyone else slows down because you've got to keep the rope the right distance between you. If one person starts moving fast, you all begin to move at the same pace.

Make sure you are building relationships with people you can pace your life with. Are you around people who are going to help you get to the summit? You can't have relationships with people who aren't going where you are going. If one goes to Mount Rainier, another to Mount

Adams and another to Mount Hood, there is no relationship, no cohesiveness, no togetherness and no unity.

If you have friends whose priority in life is money, image, boats, careers or something other than the will of God, it's going to be hard for you to be hooked up together.

How are you going to climb together if each person has a different vision? You need people you can get into relationship with, people you can work together with to reach your summit—ones who are striving to be in the center of God's will. So the number-one issue in climbing your mountain is, *Who are you roped up with?*

Proverbs 13:20 says, **He who walks with wise men will be wise, but the companion of fools will be destroyed.** Who are you hanging with? Are you hanging with a gossip? A negative, griping, complaining person? One who always has a problem or who is always upset? You've got to find some new friends if you want to climb your mountain of destiny!

"Brother Treat, you're talking about my wife!"

Listen, when we were up on the mountain, roping up and getting ready for the final ascent, our guide would not allow a husband and wife to be on the same rope, because in some situations if you can't get one out, you have to cut the rope. If it's a husband and wife, the husband might drag two or three people down because he won't cut the rope on his wife.

How many people are you dragging down because you won't cut the rope on some negative relationships? Come on, are you willing to sacrifice your life, your marriage and your kids for some dingbat who doesn't care anything about the will of God?

Someone else says, "Brother Treat, you are talking about my brother." Cut the rope! "You are talking about my neighbor." Cut it! "You're talking about my dad." Cut it quickly!

Jesus said in Matthew 10:37, **"He who loves father or mother more than Me is not worthy of Me. And he who loves son or daughter more than Me is not worthy of Me."**

You must decide, Are you going to fulfill your destiny? Are you going to reach the summit? Or are you going to play around with people who aren't going there?

"Well, Brother Treat, that's kind of a cold attitude," you might say. No, that's the will-of-God attitude! We love them, we care, we share and we minister, but we're not going to hook up if they aren't going where we are going. If we're not going the same direction, we simply cannot rope up together.

I've talked about having right relationships so many times through the years, yet again and again I've seen people dragged down into the crevasses of life because they were roped to the wrong people. I've seen them lose ministries, businesses and marriages. Their kids end up pregnant and on drugs because the parents were in wrong relationships. I am passionate about it because it is a terrible thing to see people dragged away from their destiny into a crevasse.

Several years ago, seven men on Mount Rainier fell into a crevasse. A week later, one of my friends was climbing the mountain. He walked past the place where they fell. He saw the seven skid marks of ice axes and crampons and finger marks of these men who had scratched into the snow and ice. He said, "It was a scary thing to walk past the place where these men could not stop themselves and slid to their death."

When he said that to me, I said, "I wonder how many people I've watched slide down crevasses of divorce, drugs, alcohol, sin and despair, losing their marriages, their kids and their destinies."

That's why it's so important: *Get hooked up with the right people.*

Second Corinthians 6:14 says, **Do not be unequally yoked together with unbelievers.**

I've heard people say, "Well, he said he was a Christian." Or, "She said she was a Christian." But they don't believe that God heals. They are not sure if God wants to prosper their lives. They don't spend any time in the Word, and they don't have time to be faithful in church. Those people may say they are Christians, but if they act like unbelievers, don't get roped together with them.

Be careful whom you are in relationship with. For me to hook up with you means I am giving you the opportunity to affect my life. I can't go alone, but I am going to be really careful whom I rope up with. You can't go alone, but you've got to be aware of whom you are going with.

PREPARED WITH THE GOSPEL OF PEACE

Now, there are a few things you've got to have on the mountain, like the rope, as we've mentioned, and crampons. You put crampons on your boots because when you get to frozen snow, which is crunchy and icy, you're able to drive your boots in and keep your footing.

In Ephesians 6, Paul talks about putting on your armor:

Put on the whole armor of God, that you may be able to stand against the wiles of the devil.

Take up the whole armor of God, that you may be able to withstand in the evil day, and having done all, to stand.

Stand therefore.

Ephesians 6:11,13,14

Look how many times the word *stand* appears in these verses: "*Stand* against the wiles of the devil. Take up the whole armor of God to with*stand* in the evil day. And having done all, to *stand*. *Stand* therefore."

Verse 15 says, **Having shod your feet with the preparation of the gospel of peace....** To climb to the summit, preparation means everything.

Someone once said, "You've got to have the will to win." Many people have the will to win, but they don't have the will to *prepare* to win.

You want to win, to get ahead and to get to the top so badly, but you don't want to prepare. You don't want to study. You don't want to pray. You don't want to put in the time to do what it takes to be able to go to the top. But I believe the will to prepare is rising up in you. The *motivation* and the *desire* to prepare are rising up in you. The *diligence* and *determination* are rising up in you.

What are you prepared with? You are prepared with the gospel—the Word of God, the message of Jesus Christ. If you don't have the preparation of the gospel, you will get off track and become sidetracked, distracted or tricked.

People who don't know the Word will believe unusual things and listen to strange voices.

Jesus said, "My sheep follow Me because they know My voice." (John 10:4,5,27.) When you know the Word, you know the voice of God. You must be a Word-based person to have a firm footing. Your feet must be shod with the preparation of the gospel of peace.

Let me give you another example from our climb. When we prepared to begin our descent from the summit of Mount Rainier at 10 o'clock in the morning of the third day, it was clear, and the sun began to warm everything up quickly. Yet the summit was ten degrees below freezing. The wind was blowing so hard we were all bundled up trying to stay warm.

As we came down just a few feet, the snow was softening because of the warmth of the sun. We had our crampons on and our ice axes in hand, but the snow was so soft that we began sliding. That's a scary feeling—you can't see over the edge because it's straight down, and you can't stop sliding. The snow just slides with you.

So what happens in life if you are not prepared with the Word of God? You are slipshod instead of well-shod. *Slipshod* comes from an old term used when shodding a horse. When they did a poor job, the nails didn't set well in the horse's shoe. The horse could loosen the shoe or throw it and not be able to continue to walk. It was slipshod.

Instead of being well-shod with the preparation of the gospel, many Christians are slipshod too. They are not consistent in the Word. They don't have time for the Word. They get to church once or twice a month, but they don't really apply the Word of God to their lives because they are not shod with the preparation of the gospel of peace.

What happens? They start sliding in life, and they can't stop. They see their marriages sliding, but they can't stop. They see their finances sliding, but they can't stop. They see their kids sliding, and they don't know what to do. They are frustrated and angry, but they don't know what to do to stop their marriages, finances and kids from sliding into the world.

How many people have started to slide and wanted to stop but couldn't? They aren't shod with the preparation of the gospel of peace. They get embarrassed because they've slipped down so far. They don't want to come to church because they have slipped back into the world. They don't want to be around their Christian friends because they got someone pregnant. Or their friends find out they've been dating some jerk. They find out they've been off doing some crazy stuff. Their ego holds them away, and the devil says,

"Now don't go around those Christians, because they will judge you."

A real Christian, although he won't approve, won't judge you; he'll help you. He will rope up with you to stop you from sliding.

The whole process of sliding comes when we are not well-shod and don't have our crampons on. But how do you get off a mountain when the snow becomes too soft?

The way we did it was to set these "standards" deep into the snow. We hooked a rope onto them and belayed off the mountain. When we'd get to the end of the 150-foot rope, we would set another standard and hook our harnesses to that standard. We waited for everyone to come down. The last person would bring the rope and belay down, and then we'd set another rope and climb down from that.

You can't go to the top of the mountain by yourself. You can't get out of danger by yourself. You've got to have right relationships, and your feet need to be shod with the preparation of the gospel to make it to the top in your destiny journey.

PERSONAL APPLICATION OF SUMMIT-CLIMBING TRUTHS

1. I have settled for less than God's best in the area(s) of

   _____

   _____

   _____

   I'm moving up from this area by _____

   _____

   _____

   _____

2. The thing that has kept me from God's highest life is _

   _____

   _____

   _____

   I am strategizing right now to overcome mediocrity and climb to my destiny summit by _____

   _____

   _____

   _____

3. I am roped up with _____ to keep me from falling in my spiritual climb to the summit.

4. I am building godly relationships and strengthening them by _____

    _____

    _____

    I need to cut the rope on the following relationships:

    _____

    _____

    _____

    _____

    My stability is in the gospel of peace, which I am maturing in by _____

    _____

    _____

    _____

CHAPTER NINE

LIGHTENING YOUR BACKPACK

Hebrews 12:1 says we are surrounded by a great cloud of witnesses. This is talking about the saints who have blazed the trail of life and are now in the presence of Jesus. We can complete our destiny climb because those who have gone before us did it. They set a standard for us.

Verse 1 goes on to say, **Let us lay aside every weight, and the sin which so easily ensnares us, and let us run** [climb] **with endurance** [or patience] **the race** [the mountain] **that is set before us.** Lay aside every weight. What does the marathon runner wear when he or she runs twenty-six miles? Next to nothing! I mean, those skimpy shorts and shirt carry almost no weight at all. Why? Because when you have a hard challenge, you cannot afford to carry any extra weight.

On our climb up Mount Rainier, there were some things that we had to have in our backpacks—like ropes and crampons—but there were a lot of things we didn't need.

When we went to the summit on the last day, we left every-thing we didn't need in the tent at the camp. We left it there and picked it up on our way back down Mount Rainier. You cannot make the summit with a forty-pound pack. The snow is too soft, so you've got to lighten your pack.

We needed food. If you live in the lowlands, you can live on Coke, Cheetos and Hershey bars. But if you want to climb a mountain, you'll need to eat some wholesome food. You have to watch your diet and watch what you're putting into your body. Some people don't care what goes into their body because they're not planning to go anywhere!

REMOVE FEAR

Likewise, in climbing the mountain of your destiny, there are some things you're going to have to unpack. You can't carry *fear*, for example, if you are going to your summit. What are you afraid of anyway?

"Well, Brother Treat, I'm worried about nuclear disas-ters." Listen, if there is a nuclear disaster, you won't need to worry! You can't carry fear if you are going to your summit.

What are you worried about? "I'm worried about cancer." The fear of cancer is more powerful than the cancer itself. But Jesus can heal cancer.

"I'm afraid my kids are going to get hurt." The fear of your children getting hurt is the worst because the Bible says the thing you fear will come upon you. "I'm afraid something will happen to them." Why don't you believe God? Trust God? The angels of God are encamped around about your children. No evil shall come nigh them. Quote Psalm 91 over your children.

You cannot go to the summit with fear in your pack. You have to leave it at camp. Get rid of it if you want to go to the top.

Second Timothy 1:7 says, **God has not given us a spirit of fear, but of power and of love and of a sound mind.** Where did you get that fear? You picked it up from a spirit of the world. Get it out of your pack, or you won't make it to the top.

REMOVE SMALL THINKING

Get rid of *small thinking*. Put *vision, hope* and *faith* into your pack. Include a big mind and big thoughts. You can't make it to the summit with *small thinking,* with *good enough* thinking, with *pretty good* thinking, with *okay* thinking. Get a big mind, an open mind, the vision, God's will, plan and purpose for your life.

No one who has just tried to get by has had a great life. No one has done anything great or has enjoyed this life by just trying to survive. Think big! Get out of the smallness and shake off the limitations.

Israel grieved God because they limited Him. When I stand before God on Judgment Day, the one thing I don't want to hear is, "Boy, you sure limited Me in your life."

I'll try some things that may not work and maybe I'll go over the edge a little too far, but I'd rather have God say, "You pressed the edge, didn't you? You went to the limit. You trusted Me," rather than, "You lived a small life because of your small mind." Come on, God has big stuff for us! So leave the small mind at base camp, because it won't get you to the summit.

REMOVE DOUBT

You're going to have to leave *doubt* behind too. Doubt won't get you to the summit.

"Well, I'm not sure God heals everybody." Get sure! Read His Word, which is His will.

"I'm not sure God wants to prosper everybody." Get sure! Read the Book! It will drive out the doubt.

You can't reach your summit if you are saying, "I hope it works," "I'm not sure," "You never know," "I wonder if we are on the right trail," or "I wonder if we are on the right mountain." Doubt will zap your strength.

What does a baseball player say when he steps up to the plate? He says, "I can hit this ball." He's got to believe. When the golfer steps up to the tiny white ball with the whole world watching on TV, what is he saying? "No problem. I'm going to hit this ball right into the hole." He's got to believe.

Doubt will keep you from your summit.

"Well, my granddaddy had heart failure. It's a genetic thing, you know. I mean, I could die from heart failure too," someone might say. Well, you could because of your doubt. What you have inherited is not as much physically genetic as it is spiritually genetic. You accept negative attitudes, doubts and fears and they will kill you. Leave doubt at camp, because if you are going to the summit, you can't carry it with you.

Lighten your backpack. I'm telling you, I felt so good climbing the mountain on the third day because I had carried forty pounds the first two days. The third day I was carrying under twenty pounds. That's a big difference.

REMOVE ANGER

Take *anger* out of your backpack. Do you know how hard it is to live every day with twenty or thirty pounds of anger on you? You're mad. Frustrated. Upset. Temperamental. You have a short fuse.

"Well, Brother Treat, it's because I'm Irish." No, that's not it. "It's because I'm German." No, that's not it either. "It's because I'm from Missouri." No, that's not it. You have a bad attitude and a bad temper because you've adopted a bad way of thinking.

We let ourselves get mad. Something goes wrong, and we just get mad.

The light turns red, and you sputter, "That lousy light! It makes me so mad sitting at this dumb stop light. Another red light!" Come on, you spent $100,000 of your tax money last year to put that light up there! Now you're mad because it turned red.

Everything has the ability to make a mad person mad because the "madness" is in him. When things happen around him, the anger just comes out.

Anger is like tea in a tea bag. The hot water keeps bringing out the flavor of the tea.

Now, you may be blaming your anger on the light, the traffic, your wife or husband or your kids. But as for your kids, you are the one who had the kids! You brought them into the world. And if they made you mad because they spilled milk, well, that's just part of being a kid. The anger isn't in them; it's in you. You carry it around every day. Your pack is too heavy and you are not going to make it to your destiny because you are mad, angry, upset, slamming doors, kicking the cat, stomping around and not talking.

Anger will weigh you down. Those who don't get rid of it may even die young. Some preacher will tell a lie at such a person's funeral, but it won't be me! "He was such a good person," the preacher will say. "We don't know why the Lord took him home so young."

Maybe they'll let me give a little input! I'll say, "Well, Brother so-and-so was a mad man. He got mad at the traffic, mad at his kids, mad at the dog and mad at the moles in his yard. He was just mad. And because of that, he didn't make it to his summit."

Why? Because his pack was too heavy. It was filled with anger. Don't carry anger. Take it out and leave it in the camp. Just leave it there.

REMOVE HEAVINESS AND ANXIETY

In Matthew 11:28, Jesus says, **"Come to Me, all you who labor and are heavy laden. . . ."** If you walk around upset, angry, frustrated, anxious and nervous, that's too heavy a burden for you. You can't live that way. You can't climb your summit carrying those weights. You ought to take that stuff out of your pack. You can't get to the top of life to fulfill your destiny if you are burdened down with heaviness and the like.

"Come to Me, all you who labor and are heavy laden, and I will give you rest," Jesus said (Matt. 11:28). You've got to live *light*. You've got to be a Christian *light*. Unload the heaviness.

You say, "Brother Treat, how can I? It's part of me. It's part of my demeanor. It's my heritage. Everyone I've known has been like this. How can I change it? Can I be delivered?"

No, you can't be delivered, because deliverance means we are casting an evil spirit out of you. In some cases that may be needed, but most people don't need deliverance. *They need a new way of thinking.*

You can break old habits of anger and negative thinking and speaking. You can think differently. Most of what is needed is just to make a decision: "I'm tired of being mad at the traffic, at my kids, at my wife or at my husband. I'm just going to relax and come unto Jesus."

"Take My yoke upon you and learn from Me, for I am gentle and lowly in heart, and you will find rest for your souls. For My yoke is easy and My burden is light.

Matthew 11:29,30

Don't get so serious, so frustrated or so anxious. Chill out! Take those things out of your backpack if you want to reach your summit.

REMOVE PAST FAILURES

If you're going to make it to your summit, get rid of *past failures*. Probably everyone, at one point or another, has been held back by past failures. "I don't want to try because I've tried before and I messed up." "I've got to be careful because last time I did something like this, it blew up in my face." "I've got to watch out because I stepped out before and I got fired. I ended up losing everything. I don't want to do it because it didn't work before." Now we can learn from our past, but if we allow our past failures to stop us from taking another step, we'll be ripped off!

The enemy has you right where he wants you. Usually it's young people who start new things—companies such as

Microsoft and Boeing. It's young people who birth most of the new churches in our land. Why? Many older people are afraid to try because their past failures have hung them up.

There are times when you are ready to go beyond your past failures, but the people around you won't let you. Your spouse says, "We've got to be careful. Last time you went off on something like this we lost $3,000. What are we going to do this time?" Maybe you'll lose it again, but I'd rather lose it trying to climb my mountain than to hang on to what I've got and die right there. Come on!

Past failures are very real, but you don't have to let them hinder you. Maybe the last person you dated was a jerk, but the next guy may be the right one! Don't stop all relationships just because you got hooked up with a turkey! Cut the rope, let that guy fall into the crevasse and hook up with someone else!

Some people hold back from relationships with other people because they got hurt in the past. Someone burned them. You can't let past failures keep you from your destiny. Drop that thing out of your pack. Leave it at the camp. Go on to the summit.

"Well, what if it happens again?" No, not "what if"! It *will* happen again. You will have another failure, no doubt about it. But drop it off at the camp and keep right on going. Learn to accept failure, but then leave it behind and keep right on going.

The whole process of climbing your destiny summit is learning how to control your falls. Keep pressing through your failures, and never allow past things to stop you from your future. What's worse than failing is allowing that failure to be your last.

Now Climb to Your Summit!

Unload all these things from your pack. Get rid of them. Lighten your pack. Then you are ready to climb toward your summit. Your shoulders feel good, and your pack carries just what you need. Now you are able to climb where God wants you to go.

There's a great destiny for you. It's at the top. The victory is sweet. The rejoicing is fun. The celebration is great. Settling for life in the lowlands, accepting the mediocre or stopping halfway cannot compare to going to the summit.

Make this confession with me: *In the name of Jesus, I'm climbing my mountain of transformation. I'm going to my summit. I am fulfilling my destiny. I am unloading everything I don't need, and I'm going to make it to the top of God's will for my life!*

PERSONAL APPLICATION OF SUMMIT-CLIMBING TRUTHS

1. I need to lay aside the following weights in order to pursue my destiny climb:

   _____

   _____

   _____

   _____

2. I need to *remove* the following items from my backpack to successfully complete my climb to the summit of life:

   _____

   _____

   _____

   _____

3. I need to *add* the following items to my backpack to successfully complete my climb to the summit of my destiny:

   _____

   _____

   _____

   _____

ENDNOTES

Chapter 6

[1] Strong, "Hebrew," entry #2742, p. 43.

[2] *Webster's New World College Dictionary*, 3d College Ed., s.v. "incisive" and "decisive."

[3] Strong, "Hebrew," entry #2742, p. 43.

[4] Strong, "Greek," entry #1754, p. 28.

REFERENCES

Strong, James. *Strong's Exhaustive Concordance of the Bible.* "Hebrew and Chaldee Dictionary," "Greek Dictionary of the New Testament." Nashville: Abingdon, 1890.

Webster's New World College Dictionary, 3d College Ed. New York: Macmillan General Reference, 1986.

About the Author

Casey Treat pastors one of the largest churches in the Pacific Northwest—Christian Faith Center—in Seattle, Washington. He is an outstanding minister, author and motivational speaker. Pastor Treat is also the founder of Dominion College in Seattle, serves on the board of directors of Church Growth International (founded by Dr. David Yonggi Cho in Seoul, Korea) and is a co-founding trustee of Oral Roberts' International Charismatic Bible Ministries. His daily program, *Living on Course,* can be seen on cable and over the air stations daily from coast to coast. He is the founder of Vision Ministries Fellowship. And his many books and tape series have helped thousands internationally.

Casey and his wife, Wendy, reside in the Seattle area with their three children.

To contact Casey Treat,

write:

Casey Treat

P.O. Box 98800

Seattle, WA 98198

Please include your prayer requests

and comments when you write.

OTHER BOOKS BY CASEY TREAT

Living the New Life

God's Word for Every Circumstances

Blueprint for Life

You Can Pull Down Strongholds and Break Old Habits

Love, Sex & Kids

Fulfilling Your God-Given Destiny

Renewing the Mind: The Foundation for Your Success

Available from your local bookstore.

HARRISON HOUSE
Tulsa, Oklahoma 74153

THE HARRISON HOUSE VISION

Proclaiming the truth and the power

Of the Gospel of Jesus Christ

With excellence;

Challenging Christians to

Live victoriously,

Grow spiritually,

Know God intimately.